THE FLAME

by

Edmund Banyard

No performance of this play may be given without the written permission of the publisher to whom all applications for performing rights should be made, enclosing a reply paid envelope.

The performance time is approximately 25 minutes

Published by:
National Christian Education Council
Robert Denholm House
Nutfield
Redhill RH1 4HW

Published for:
RADIUS
Christ Church and Upton Chapel
Kennington Road
London SE1 7QP

British Library Cataloguing-In-Publication Data:
Banyard, Edmund
The Flame.
I. Title
822.914

ISBN 0-7197-0709-9

A co-operative venture in Christian drama by NCEC and RADIUS

Series Editors: Silvia Read and William Fry

RADIUS is the shortened name of the Religious Drama Society of Great Britain, bringing together amateur and professional actors, writers, and others involved in religion and the performing arts.

RADIUS exists to encourage all drama which throws light on the human condition especially through a Christian understanding. It aims to help local congregations to a deeper appreciation of all types of drama, to inform them of opportunities to see work of a high quality, to give the technical advice and assistance needed for a good standard of local productions, and to help them to find ways of introducing the lively arts into their worship.

The Society runs a unique lending library, organises an annual summer school, holds regular play-writing competitions and publishes its own magazine.

First published 1980

This edition published 1990

Typesetting by One and a Half Graphics, Redhill, Surrey.
Printed in Great Britain by Halstan & Co. Ltd, Amersham, Bucks.

CONTENTS

		Page
	PRODUCTION NOTES	4
	DRAMATIS PERSONÆ	4
SCENE 1	The Coming of the Flame; A Moment in Time	5
SCENE 2	The Lighting of the Torches; The Next Stage	12
SCENE 3	The Undying Fire; Happy Ever After?	15

THE FLAME

PRODUCTION NOTES

This play is a one-act fantasy parable in the style of the Theatre of the Absurd. Four ordinary people are offered a flame to light the World. They promptly form into a committee and agree to bury the flame in a fireplace as a lasting memorial to the donor, but they cannot get rid of it so easily.

DRAMATIS PERSONÆ

CHARACTER ONE	(who is male)
CHARACTER TWO	(who is female)
CHARACTER THREE	(who is female)
CHARACTER FOUR	(who is male)
ANGELO	(who can be male

SCENE 1

The Coming of the Flame; a Moment in Time

Four characters are sitting facing the audience. To begin with, they are speaking more to the audience than to each other.

ONE *(Rather listlessly)* This morning I got up.

TWO I got up this morning.

THREE *(A more forceful character)* We all got up. *(Looking at FOUR)* I said, we all got up!

FOUR Oh yes, most certainly, you're quite right. Yes, yes, we all got up.

ONE I had cornflakes. Hot milk makes them rather soggy. perhaps I ought to try cold milk for a change.

TWO Two slices of toast and black coffee for my breakfast; always the same.

THREE I think we may take it that we all had breakfast. *(Looking at FOUR)* Didn't we?

FOUR Well, as a matter of fact, I only …

ONE I caught my usual train. It was late of course, and crowded.

TWO I work in a shop.

THREE Naturally we all went to work.

FOUR I didn't go to work today.

THREE You didn't? Why not?

FOUR I took a day's sick leave.

THREE What's wrong with you?

FOUR Nothing. I wanted to get on with painting the house.

ONE I've been doing exactly the same job for the last five years.

TWO We didn't have many customers. Not like the sales, we're run off our feet then.

THREE I had a very busy day. I always have a busy day.

FOUR I might just as well have gone to work.

THREE Why?

FOUR It rained.

ONE	This evening I watched the tele.
TWO	I started to watch the tele, but I fell asleep.
THREE	I've got too much to do to watch the tele. Anyway, it was all repeats.
FOUR	I went to the Pub. I'd been watching the tele all day.
ONE	It's nearly time to go to bed.
TWO	Another day almost finished.
THREE	There's someone coming!
ONE	At this hour?
TWO	I don't like meeting new people.
THREE	He's carrying a torch; it's giving a very good light.

FOUR *(Who has almost dozed off)* You going? Oh, a very good night to you.

THREE	Not goodnight! Wash your ears out! There's a man coming with a torch, can't you see him?
FOUR	I say! Yes! Isn't it lovely! I wish I had one.

ANGELO *(Entering)* Why not?

FOUR	You mean that I could have one?
ANGELO	This flame is to be shared.
TWO	With anybody?
ONE	There'll be a charge of course, there is sure to be a charge. Even when it says, 'Send no money now', you always have to pay later.
ANGELO	There is no charge.
THREE	I don't like the sound of this at all. There's something fishy about it. You don't get anything for nothing in this world. Now tell us straight, where did you get it?
ANGELO	It was given to me at the border.
ONE	The border?
TWO	Which border?
THREE	I thought so! It's foreign!
ANGELO	It was given to me at the border where time meets eternity.
FOUR	That sounds lovely, I don't understand it of course, but it sounds lovely.
ONE	D'you know, I think I would like to share the flame.
TWO	And so would I.

THREE — I give up, I really do! There you go, rushing into things you know nothing about. 'Got it at the border where time meets eternity.' What is that supposed to mean?

ANGELO — Have you ever stood on the threshold of eternity. *(It is obvious that she hasn't)* I found myself there with a deep longing in my heart, suddenly I heard a voice, 'Will you carry the undying flame back to the world of men and women?' and I found myself saying, 'I will'. But I didn't know where to find the flame or how to carry it, so I stood wondering what I should do when the voice spoke again, 'You have a torch, lift it up,' and I found that I had got a torch though I'd never noticed it before. So I took the torch and held it up and suddenly it was alight.

FOUR — Why look, I've got a torch! I often wondered what this was, but of course, it's a torch!

THREE — Put that thing away for goodness sake! Why, you don't even know whether it is safe.

ANGELO — Safe? If you mean, is it completely predictable? Can you be sure of controlling it? The answer is no, it is not safe. No flame that comes from the threshold of eternity can be safe.

THREE — You see what I mean.

ONE — If we find our torches and you light them, how do we keep them alight?

TWO — Yes, what do we do for fuel?

ANGELO — That is both the easiest and the hardest thing of all. Whenever your torch burns low you just hold it high, exposed to the winds of heaven, and it renews itself.

ONE — For ever?

ANGELO — For ever.

FOUR — Would you light my torch?

ONE — I think I have one ...

TWO — And so have I ...

THREE — There you go again! Now, I'm not against you having lighted torches, indeed I will probably have one myself as a gesture of solidarity; but if we are going to do this thing at all at least let us do it properly. We must form a committee.

FOUR Must we form a committee?

THREE We must do things decently and in order. *(To ONE, TWO and FOUR in turn)* Now if you sit here, you here, and you there. *(They are now all gathered around a table, THREE is Chairman and TWO is Secretary. THREE now addresses ANGELO)* I think that you had better wait over there.

ANGELO But all I wish to do is …

THREE *(Rapping on the table)* Order, order. Let us have the minutes of the last meeting.

TWO As this is the first meeting we haven't got any.

THREE Oh, very well, we shall have to do without them. We'll have them next time.

FOUR *(To ONE)* She's an awfully good chairman you know, runs the meeting very efficiently.

ONE *(Quite seriously)* Yes, and doesn't let people confuse things by introducing new ideas.

THREE If I may have your attention, thank you! We are here to consider the offer of a flame to light what we are told are torches.

FOUR I move that we accept the offer.

THREE Do you mind? I haven't finished.

TWO *(Also seriously)* Do you want that minuted?

THREE Just the main points. Now the questions before us are one, do we want to accept the offer made by Mr … er … I didn't catch your name?

ANGELO Angelo.

TWO How do you spell it?

THREE A.N.G.E.L.O., I expect. It's not British.

TWO A.N.G.E. …

THREE L.O. Angelo. Have you got it now?

TWO Yes, thank you.

THREE As I was saying, the first question is, do we want to accept this offer of Mr … er … Angelo's, and secondly, if we do, what do we do with the torches when they are lit?

FOUR Can I move a resolution now?

THREE Really! Still, if you must.

FOUR Then I move that we accept Mr Angelo's kind offer and ask him to light our torches straight away.

ONE I second that.

THREE Is there any amendment? Does anybody want to speak to the motion? Then we shall vote on it, though I would suggest that you delete the words 'straight away', they make it sound a little precipitate. You agree? Good. Then in that amended form I put it to the meeting. Those in favour? *(Three hands go up)* Any to the contrary? The motion is carried.

ONE, TWO and FOUR start to get up.

FOUR Here is my torch ...

THREE Come back! We haven't finished! There is the rest of the agenda. *(They sit down again)* The next question is, what do we do with the flame when we have got it?

FOUR Mr Angelo said we should carry it with us.

THREE 'Mr Angelo said!' Have you considered how inconvenient that might be?

ONE Inconvenient?

THREE Carrying a flame around all the time; inconvenient and risky. You heard him say that it wasn't safe.

TWO Is that right for 'inconvenient'?

THREE 'I' before the 'E' dear.

FOUR But what else can we do?

THREE I thought you might come to asking that.

ONE Well, what else *can* we do?

THREE *(With a note of satisfaction)* Build a fireplace so that we can put it where it will be really safe.

FOUR A fireplace?

THREE Yes, a fireplace. If this is indeed a flame from the threshold of eternity, the last thing we want is for it to be carted around willy nilly, in a risky way to get into the hands of every Jimmy or Jemina. I tremble to think what might happen. We have agreed to have our torches lit, I accept that: but my proposal now is that they should then be set in a fireplace where they can be properly controlled.

ANGELO — But the flame is meant to be exposed!

THREE — Mr Angelo, we are most grateful to you for bringing the flame, but you understand, don't you, you are not actually a member of the committee. I'm sure you agree that we must do things properly, so if you don't mind …

ONE — Are you quite sure that we ought to build a fireplace?

THREE — Now what could be better than a really well-designed and well-built fireplace? Not only would it keep the flame safe, it would also let everybody know just how important the flame really is.

FOUR — Of course, if you put it like that …

ONE — I hadn't thought of it that way.

TWO — Nor had I.

THREE — You see the point now though? Good. Then I propose that when our torches are lighted we put them carefully together and build a fireplace around them. Is that seconded. *(There is a nod)* All in favour?

TWO — Proposed from the Chair and carried. Is that right?

THREE — There is an 'O' in unanimous dear. Now there is no other business I trust. So, date of next meeting. Same time, same day, next month? Good. I declare the meeting closed. *(The committee breaks up. As they go THREE moves over to ANGELO)*

ANGELO — But you ….

THREE — Ah, Mr Angelo, I'm glad to be able to tell you that we have accepted your kind offer. Now we must arrange an appropriate ceremony for lighting our torches. It is so important that we do things decently and in order, don't you think? I'll be in touch with you. Good night.

ANGELO sings. Meanwhile the others set the stage for the next scene. There is the beginning of the Fireplace. The proceedings will be reminiscent of a church service with FOUR presiding.

ANGELO *(Sings 'Cry to the Winds')*

Recorder (optional)

Andante espressivo

Cry to the Winds

Words: Edmund Banyard
Music: Roy Wise

END OF SCENE 1

SCENE 2

The Lighting of the Torches; The Next Stage

FOUR — We are met together on this solemn and joyful occasion that we may firstly … er … that we may have our torches kindled by the flame brought to us by our dear brother *(Beckoning him to come)* Angelo. And then, secondly, that we may place them for safe keeping in this spot *(It takes him a moment to find it)* where shall be raised a Fireplace to endure for all generations.

TWO — I think Three would have done it better.

ONE — She couldn't possibly do it.

TWO — Why?

ONE — Not a woman's job.

FOUR — Now I will call upon our brother Angelo to address a few words to us.

ANGELO — My friends, my very dear friends, I am asked for a few words, but are there any words in the whole of your language with which I can make you understand, even now, that you are making a mistake, a most terrible mistake.

TWO — He says that we are making a mistake.

THREE — Don't pay any attention dear. It's only a sermon, it's not meant to be taken seriously.

ANGELO — I will gladly share with you the flame that was given to me for that is why I have been sent; but that flame is for carrying in the world, to be held high, to be fanned by the winds of heaven that all may see it and be glad.

TWO — All this talk of flames has made me wonder whether I lit the oven before I came out.

ONE — Too late to worry now.

TWO — But what shall we do for lunch? No, I think I do remember lighting it.

ONE — Oh good!

TWO — But did I put the joint in?

ANGELO — I know that carrying the flame into the world can be a risky business. There will be times when it will be hated because people want to do things that can only be done in darkness. There will be other times when the flame starts new fires in unexpected places. But take the risks, I beg you, do not bury the flame in a fireplace, however beautiful it may be; carry it with you wherever you go, for only so can the world receive the light that it needs.

FOUR Amen. *(This is echoed by ONE, TWO and THREE)*

FOUR Now we come to the solemn moment of the lighting of the torches.

ANGELO has his lighted torch and each of the others, beginning with FOUR, come to him to have their torches lit. To each in turn he speaks as he lights their torch.

ANGELO Carry your torch into the world and hold it high that all may see the light that has been given to you.

Each in turn responds 'I will so do', but nevertheless goes and puts it in the Fireplace.

FOUR Now we will sing, 'Come all you men and women' and as we sing it there will be a collection to help with the next stage of the building of the Fireplace. A good start has been made and we must build on that foundation in a worthy manner so do please give generously.

ONE, TWO, THREE and FOUR sing to the tune Aurelia (The Church's One Foundation)

ONE, TWO, THREE & FOUR *(Sing)*

Come all you men and women
Rejoice with us today
We've started on the Fireplace
The work is under way
The hearth is in position
The chimney's working fine
O come and join us building
A Fireplace for all time. Amen

FOUR comes out with ANGELO.

FOUR My dear fellow, how can I thank you for all that you've done for us? Such an impressive occasion and such stirring words. It has done us all a power of good. You are of course our Patron and this Fireplace will be your memorial for all time.

ANGELO I do not want a memorial!

FOUR Your modesty is most becoming my dear fellow, but you must allow us to know best … excuse me one moment … *(He turns to call to the others)* This way, this way! *(He begins speaking again to ANGELO)* Now at the celebration dinner I thought perhaps you might … *(But ANGELO has gone)*

ONE I thought Mr Angelo was with you.

FOUR He was a moment ago, but …

TWO Probably got some other appointment.

THREE Well we can't hang about, mustn't keep the caterers waiting.

FOUR Quite so, quite so. *(As they go)* What a strange chap to be sure.

ANGELO returns to sing again

The players complete the structure and leave. There is now a fine fireplace bearing the legend, 'The Angelo Memorial Fireplace'. As ANGELO finishes his song he exits behind it. There is no fire, only one small candle burning on the mantelpiece. Centuries have passed.

END OF SCENE 2

SCENE 3

The Undying Fire; Happy Ever After?

FOUR *(Entering with ONE)* You know, I always look forward to this festival, I find it most moving. It's the sense of continuity with the past. To think of people, no doubt very much like us, laying the foundations all those hundreds of years ago.

ONE D'you think that we, the principal trustees I mean, could have a word together before the ceremony?

FOUR If you say so, my dear chap; nothing wrong I hope?

TWO *(Entering with THREE)* I do hope we're not late.

THREE Parking gets worse every day. D'you know, the whole car-park is occupied by tourists.

FOUR We have become very popular in these last few years, very popular indeed.

THREE I'm sure that the commendation we received from the Historic Fireplaces Commission has had a lot to do with it.

FOUR No doubt at all.

ONE If I might break in, there's a matter I really must share with you.

THREE Business?

ONE If you don't mind. Perhaps we could sit here.

They group informally.

THREE What's all this about?

ONE This morning I have received a rather disquieting report from the consultant architects.

FOUR I thought they were very satisfied with the state of the structure.

ONE They are … in a way.

THREE What do you mean by 'in a way a'?

ONE It is not exactly the structure …

THREE Stop beating about the bush. What is the matter?

ONE From time to time, as I think you know, there has been a problem with heat, as though there were some hidden fire deep within the Fireplace.

FOUR It is quite absurd of course.

TWO I wonder …

THREE Wonder what?

TWO Oh, nothing.

THREE Come on, out with it.

TWO Well, I wonder whether … no, it's of no importance.

ONE *(Glad the interruption is now over)* The ground has been tested three times in the last fifty years to my certain knowledge and all is perfectly normal, and yet the problem is undoubtedly there, not all the time of course; but just when you think it has been finally solved, up it comes again.

FOUR Didn't we take some action about ten years back?

ONE Yes, the whole foundations were covered with a deep layer of specially hardened reinforced concrete.

TWO Why did you do that?

ONE To cut off any possible air supply.

THREE I clearly remember it, and we received a report that it was completely effective.

ONE So it seemed, so it seemed.

FOUR And now?

ONE You must understand that the concrete is very tough, very tough indeed. A good deal harder than granite.

FOUR Then there should be no trouble.

ONE But there is! It is breaking up! Just as if someone were smashing it; the air is getting in and the temperature is rising.

THREE If someone is interfering with it we must act at once.

TWO *(Hesitantly)* Do you think it is possible that there *should* be heat?

FOUR Whatever are you talking about?

TWO Doesn't the traditional story tell of Angelo bringing a flame? Perhaps we ought to be encouraging it to burn instead of stifling it.

FOUR But we have a flame. *(He points to the candle on the mantelpiece)* We tend it most carefully.

TWO But, suppose instead of the symbolic flame we should have a real blaze?

ONE — I don't think we should start a theological discussion.

THREE — Certainly not, let's be practical. Obviously vandals are at work. We must stop them immediately.

ONE — I'm quite sure that it isn't vandals. I tried hitting a piece of concrete this morning with a large sledge hammer and it made no impression at all. And yet an hour later there were new cracks. I find it all most disturbing.

THREE — What do the architects suggest?

ONE — They want us to install a cooling system. It will be very expensive. I'm sorry to have to tell you all this so abruptly, but I wanted to warn you before the formal meeting.

FOUR — This is really most disconcerting. We shall obviously have to do something about it. However, we must not let it interfere with the anniversary. *(To THREE)* I believe that you are going to propose the toast this year.

TWO — What was that? I thought I heard something.

They all listen.

TWO — Sorry, I must have been mistaken, I thought I heard singing from the Fireplace.

Pitying looks are cast in her direction. ONE is now passing the wine round.

FOUR — Are we ready? *(Nods to THREE)*

THREE — It is my privilege today to propose the toast on the occasion of this, our Patronal Festival. We are a people rooted in history, with traditions and customs which have stood the test of time. We have both moulded our heritage and been moulded by it. Today we celebrate one of our most hallowed institutions, and in particular its originator. We salute the vision and the genius that gave to us the edifice of which we are now the custodians.

There are general murmurs of approval from FOUR and ONE.

In proposing the toast to the undying memory of our Patron, the only founder and provider of the Fireplace, I dare to add the hope that the source of heat which troubles us at this moment may soon be discovered and extinguished once and for all, as over the centuries other problems have been successfuly dealt with.

More 'hear, hears!'

Then we may be sure that the Angelo Memorial Fireplace will continue to stand as a glory, a monument and a testimony to generations as yet unborn.

OTHERS Bravo, bravo, hear hear!

THREE Ladies and gentlemen, I give you the immortal memory of Angelo!

ONE, FOUR
THREE Angelo!

They drink the toast not noticing that TWO is standing looking at the Fireplace with the wine untasted.

ONE I congratulate you. You have surpassed yourself, a truly memorable toast.

FOUR Excellent, excellent. And now we really must be on our way. *(As they go)* A really remarkable speech.

Only TWO remains. Now the song is definitely heard, getting louder.

TWO I *did* hear it.

ANGELO appears and finishes the verse.

TWO That is a strange song you are singing.

ANGELO To me the most natural song in the world.

TWO Who are you?

ANGELO Does it matter who I am? I am the voice that finds an echo in your heart, isn't that enough?

TWO *(Accusingly)* You have been breaking up the Fireplace.

ANGELO No, I assure you, even though I might wish to do so I have no power.

TWO No power?

ANGELO No power.

TWO Then who has?

ANGELO Do you really want to know?

TWO Of course I do.

ANGELO Are you sure?

TWO Yes, I *must* know.

ANGELO Then you shall. It is you.

TWO I don't believe it.

ANGELO I think you do.

two But …

ANGELO You do, don't you?

TWO But how could it be me?

ANGELO By questioning the value of a fireplace without fire you made it possible for the flame to break out again.

TWO This is awful. I have had dreams, nightmares, but … I must go away, quickly, before anybody else finds out.

ANGELO Why?

TWO What else can I do?

ANGELO I think you know.

TWO I can't, I daren't.

ANGELO Plunge your hand into the crack that has opened up, pull out a torch and carry it with you into the world.

TWO *(Halffacetiously)* And what would the great Angelo say to my doing that to his Fireplace? *(Realising)* Oh no!

ANGELO has begun to sing again. TWO starts towards the Fireplace, hesitates, becomes aware of the drink in her hand, lifts it towards ANGELO and drinks. Then putting down the glass she kneels by the Fireplace, plucks out a torch and carries it through the audience while he is completing the song. The lights fade.

Alternatively TWO could carry the lighted torch to the audience and kindle other lights for members of the audience to carry out with them.

THE END